BUDDHIST PROVERBS

BOOK II

PUBLISHED

BY

MAHAMAKUT EDUCATIONAL COUNCIL

THE BUDDHIST UNIVERSITY OF THAILAND

First Edition B.E. 2501

8/-

Wachirayān Warōrot, Prince Patriarch of Thailand, 1859-1921.

FOREWORD

This book has for years been used as a text-book for the newcomers of the Buddhist Order of Thailand and also for the laity who are interested in the study of Buddhism. Its translation is now completed by one of our graduates with the approval of our lecturers in Buddhism. The Mahamakuta Foundation, with a view to making it better known to foreigners, is presenting it to the English-reading public and hopes that the more it is widely studied and put to practice the better it will contribute to the cause of inner peace, both to the individuals and to the nations as a whole.

Mahamakuta Educational Council
September 9, B. E. 2501.

คำนำ

หนังสือพุทธศาสนสุภาษิต เล่ม ๒ นี้ ทางคณะสงฆ์แห่งประเทศไทยได้ใช้เป็นหลักสูตรนักธรรมชั้นโท และใช้แพร่หลายทั่วไป ในสังฆมณฑลทั้งภายในประเทศและนอกประเทศที่ใกล้เคียงเป็นเวลานานมาแล้ว ทางมูลนิธิมหามกุฏราชวิทยาลัยมีความปรารถนาเป็นอย่างยิ่งที่จะเผยแผ่ให้หนังสือนี้แพร่หลายเจริญยิ่งขึ้น ถึงต่างประเทศที่ห่างไกลออกไปอีก เพราะหนังสือเช่นนี้เป็นแนวทางแห่งสันติ เมื่อเผยแผ่ไปได้มากเพียงไรสันติธรรม ก็ย่อมเกิดขึ้นมากเพียงนั้น แต่ที่ยังเป็นไปตามความปรารถนานั้นไม่ได้ ก็เพราะยังขัดข้องอยู่ด้วยเหตุหลายประการ บัดนี้พระมหาสมฤทธิ์ สมิทฺธิ ป. ธ. ๖ น. ธ. เอก ศาสนศาสตร์-บัณฑิต วัดบรมนิวาส นักศึกษารุ่นที่ ๒ ของสภาการศึกษามหามกุฏราชวิทยาลัยในพระบรมราชูปถัมภ์ ปัจจุบันเป็นอาจารย์ประจำในวิชาภาษาอังกฤษในสถาบันการศึกษาแห่งนี้ ได้พยายามแปลเป็นภาษาต่างประเทศสำเร็จขึ้นอีกเรื่องหนึ่ง และถวายให้เป็นสมบัติของสภาการศึกษามหามกุฏราชวิทยาลัย อันเป็นกิจการส่วนหนึ่งของมูลนิธิมหามกุฏ ฯ ด้วย

หนังสือเล่มนี้ คุณสุชีพ ปุญญานุภาพ และคุณศิริ พุธศุกร ได้ช่วยตรวจแก้ด้วยความเอาใจใส่

สภาการศึกษามหามกุฏราชวิทยาลัยในพระบรมราชูปถัมภ์ จึงขออนุโมทนาทั้งในความพยายามและกุศลเจตนาของพระมหาสมฤทธิ์ คุณสุชีพ และคุณศิริ นั้น ผู้เช่นนี้ชื่อว่าได้ช่วยทำกิจพระศาสนา ถ้าพระสัมมาสัมพุทธเจ้ายังทรงพระชนม์อยู่ก็จักทรงอนุโมทนาสาธุการมิใช่น้อย

กิจที่ได้ทำนี้ก็เป็นเครื่องอุปถัมภ์แก่ผู้ทำนั่นเอง นึกถึงเมื่อใดก็จักอิ่มใจเมื่อนั้น และทั้งได้ใช้วิชาที่ได้จากสภาการศึกษาฯ มาทำประโยชน์ให้แก่สภาการศึกษาฯ จักปีติอิ่มใจทุกเมื่อที่ระลึกถึง

ขอกุศลส่วนนี้จงตามสนองผู้ประกอบเรื่องนี้ ให้มีความสุข ความเจริญรุ่งเรือง มั่นคงยั่งยืน ในพระธรรมของพระสัมมาสัมพุทธเจ้า เพื่อเป็นกำลังของหมู่คณะ เป็นศรีของชาติ และพระศาสนาตลอดกาลนานเทอญ.

ประธานกรรมการ

สภาการศึกษามหามกุฏราชวิทยาลัย

๑๑ ก. ย. ๒๕๐๑

คำปรารภ

ทุกครั้งที่มีพิธีประสาธน์ปริญญาบัตรแก่ภิกษุนักศึกษาของสภาการศึกษามหามกุฏราชวิทยาลัยในพระบรมราชูปถัมภ์ สภาการศึกษา ฯ มีหนังสือซึ่งจัดพิมพ์ขึ้น ที่ภิกษุผู้สำเร็จการศึกษา ผ่านการอบรมแล้ว และมีสิทธิที่จะรับปริญญาศาสนศาสตรบัณฑิต ได้แปลหรือเรียบเรียงให้แก่กรรมการสภาการศึกษา ฯ และแก่ท่านผู้มาร่วมในพิธี เพื่อแสดงว่าภิกษุนักศึกษาในรุ่นนั้น มีความรู้ความสามารถควรแก่อันที่จะได้รับปริญญาบัตรหรือไม่ ในพิธีประสาธน์ปริญญาครั้งที่แล้ว ได้ปฏิบัติอย่างนี้ แม้ในครั้งนี้ก็ได้ปฏิบัติอย่างเดียวกัน

หนังสือที่ภิกษุนักศึกษาผู้จะเข้ารับปริญญาได้จัดทำขึ้นชุดนี้ คือ หนังสือพุทธศาสนสุภาษิต แปลเป็นอังกฤษทั้งสามเล่ม และเพื่อความเหมาะสม ได้จัดพิมพ์ภาษาบาลีในพุทธศาสนสุภาษิต ด้วยอักษรโรมันแทนอักษรไทย เล่มนี้เป็นเล่มสอง ซึ่งพระมหาสมฤทธิ สมิทฺธิ ป. ธ. ๖ น. ธ. เอก ศ. บ. สำนักวัดบรมนิวาสเป็นผู้แปลเป็นอังกฤษ และใช้อักษรโรมันแทนอักษรไทย สำหรับภาษาบาลีในพุทธศาสนสุภาษิต

หนังสือ พุทธศาสนสุภาษิตภาคอังกฤษเล่มนี้ได้ผ่านการตรวจแก้จากอาจารย์สุชีพ ปุญญานุภาพ และอาจารย์ศิริ พุธศุกร ซึ่งเป็นอาจารย์ในสภาการศึกษา ฯ แล้ว และได้เคยจัดพิมพ์แล้วครั้งหนึ่ง เมื่อ พ.ศ. ๒๔๙๙ เนื่องในงานพระราชทานเพลิงพระบรมศพสมเด็จพระพันวัสสา-

อัยยิกาเจ้า โดยมหามกุฏราชวิทยาลัยเป็นผู้จัดพิมพ์ แต่หนังสือชุดนั้นได้หมดไปเสียตั้งแต่ตอนงานพระศพแล้ว

ความสำเร็จครั้งนี้นอกจากจะเป็นความสำเร็จของสภาการศึกษาฯ แล้ว ยังเป็นความสำเร็จของภิกษุไทยและของการศึกษาทางพระปริยัติธรรมในประเทศไทยอีกด้วย

พระราชสุมนต์มุนี

เลขาธิการ

สภาการศึกษามหามกุฏราชวิทยาลัย

๒๗ สิงห์ ๒๕๐๑

คำชี้แจง

หนังสือพุทธศาสนสุภาษิต มี ๓ เล่ม ใช้เป็นหลักสูตรสำหรับนักธรรม ชั้นตรี, โท และเอก ตามลำดับ เล่มแรก สมเด็จพระมหาสมณเจ้า กรมพระยาวชิรญาณวโรรส ทรงรวบรวมและแปล เล่มที่ ๒ และเล่มที่ ๓ คณะกรรมการกองตำรามหามกุฏราชวิทยาลัย รวบรวมและแปล.

เมื่อตั้งสภาการศึกษาขึ้น อบรมภิกษุสามเณรในรูปมหาวิทยาลัยพุทธศาสนา สภาการศึกษาจึงมอบหมายให้ภิกษุสามเณรผู้สำเร็จการศึกษาชั้นสูง จะรับปริญญาตรี ได้ช่วยกันแต่งและแปลตำราต่าง ๆ ดังได้ทำมาแล้วในรุ่นแรก ครั้นถึงรุ่นที่ ๒ ได้มอบให้พระมหาประยงค์ กิตฺติธโร วัดราชประดิษฐ์ ฯ พระมหาสมฤทธิ์ สมิทฺธิ วัดบรมนิวาส และพระมหาชำรง คุณนฺธโร วัดเทพศิรินทราวาส รับหน้าที่แปลหนังสือพุทธศาสนสุภาษิต เล่ม ๑,๒ และ ๓ ตามลำดับ เป็นภาษาอังกฤษ พร้อมทั้งให้เขียนภาษาบาลีเป็นอักษรโรมันพิมพ์กำกับไว้ด้วย.

เมื่อนักศึกษาทั้ง ๓ รูป จัดทำคำแปลและเขียนอักษรโรมันสำเร็จแล้ว สภาการศึกษาจึงได้มอบให้คุณศิริ พุธศุกร อาจารย์สอนภาษาอังกฤษ ผู้มีความรู้ภาษาบาลีและพระพุทธศาสนา เป็นผู้ตรวจแก้ทั้งคำแปลและอักษรโรมัน เล่มที่ ๓ ได้จัดพิมพ์ไปแล้ว คราวนี้จึงจัดพิมพ์เล่มที่ ๒ ซึ่งพระมหาสมฤทธิ์ สมิทฺธิ วัดบรมนิวาส เป็นผู้แปล.

และเมื่อปรารภที่จะพิมพ์ใช้เป็นตำราถาวรต่อไป ทางสภาการ-ศึกษาจึงขอให้ข้าพเจ้าตรวจแก้อีกครั้งหนึ่ง. โดยเหตุที่ คุณศิริ พุธศุกร เป็นผู้แก้ไขมาแต่เดิม ข้าพเจ้าจึงเชิญคุณศิริให้มาร่วมพิจารณาด้วย โดยอ่านสอบทานทุกตัวอักษร และพยายามแก้ไขให้คำแปลภาษาอังกฤษใกล้เคียงกับความในภาษาบาลีให้มากเท่าที่จะทำได้. ในการนี้คุณศิริ พุธศุกร ได้ช่วยเป็นธุระร่วมมือด้วยอย่างเป็นประโยชน์ยิ่ง ทั้งในการแก้ไขและในการตรวจปรู๊ฟ ซึ่งต้องใช้เวลาประชุมกันเกือบทุกวันเป็นเวลาเดือนเศษ.

เพื่อที่จะให้ท่านผู้อ่าน ได้ทราบรายละเอียดบางประการ ในปัญหาเรื่องจัดทำหนังสือนี้ จึงขอชี้แจงไว้ในที่นี้ด้วยเป็นข้อ ๆ คือ:—

๑. เฉพาะพระพุทธภาษิตข้อแรก อาจทำให้คนเข้าใจผิดว่า สอนให้เห็นแก่ตัวจนไม่นึกถึงประโยชน์คนอื่น จึงต้องเพิ่มเติมคำอธิบายเล่าเรื่องมูลเหตุที่ตรัสเตือนให้เร่งปฏิบัติธรรมะ ไม่ใช่มัวแต่พูดกัน.

๒. คำแปลฉบับภาษาอังกฤษ ในบางกรณีชัดกว่าภาษาไทย เพราะในภาษาไทยแปลทับศัพท์ไว้ ซึ่งผู้ไม่คุ้นกับศัพท์ทางศาสนาอาจไม่เข้าใจดีนัก แต่เมื่ออ่านเทียบเคียงกันจะเข้าใจชัดขึ้น. ขอยกตัวอย่างดังนี้:—

ข้อ ๕๒. "คนมีตัณหาเป็นเพื่อนสอง ท่องเที่ยวอยู่สู่ความเป็นอย่างนี้ และความเป็นอย่างอื่นสิ้นกาลนาน ไม่ล่วงพ้นสงสารไปได้"

๕๒ "Long is the wandering over the states of being this and being that, when a person is befriended by craving. Never can he go beyond the cycle of rebirths."

คำว่า ตัณหา เมื่อแปลว่า craving และสังสาร แปลว่า the cycle of rebirths ความก็ชัดขึ้น เพราะบางครั้ง คำว่า ตัณหา คนเข้าใจเพียงเรื่องกามารมณ์ และคำว่า สังสาร เข้าใจไปในทางเอ็นดูเห็นอกเห็นใจ แต่ความหมายในทางพระพุทธศาสนา ตัณหา หมายถึงความทะยานอยากทุกชนิด และสังสาร หมายถึงความเวียนว่ายตายเกิด.

ในข้อ ๖๔ คำว่า นามกาย อาจทำให้เข้าใจไปว่า จิตกับกาย ความจริงหมายถึง กลุ่มแห่งธรรมที่เป็นฝ่ายจิตใจ (มีเวทนา ความรู้สึก สุขทุกข์ สัญญา ความจำ เป็นต้น) คือ กาย ในที่นี้ไม่ได้แปลว่า ร่างกาย หากแปลว่า กอง, กลุ่ม หรือ หมวด, หมู่ เมื่ออ่านดูฉบับแปลเป็นอังกฤษ ที่ว่า mental compound ก็พอจะเห็นความหมายขึ้นมาบ้าง.

ข้อใน ๖๕ คำว่า "อินทรีย์ของมนุษย์ มีอยู่เพื่อประโยชน์และมิใช่ประโยชน์ คือที่ไม่รักษา ไม่เป็นประโยชน์ ที่รักษาจึงเป็นประโยชน์" นั้น เนื่องจากหนังสือนี้เป็นหลักสูตรสำหรับนักธรรมชั้นโท การแปลทับศัพท์อินทรีย์ จึงไม่ยุ่งยากสำหรับนักศึกษา แต่สำหรับคนทั่วไป อาจจะไม่ชัดพอ เมื่ออ่านฉบับอังกฤษที่ว่า

"Human sense-organs can be either useful or useless.

Those uncontroled are useless while those controled are useful." ดังนี้ ความก็ชัดขึ้น ว่า อินทรีย์ ในที่นี้หมายถึงเครื่องรับรู้ทางประสาทสัมผัส มีตา หู เป็นต้น.

อนึ่ง การแปลพุทธศาสนสุภาษิต เป็นภาษาอังกฤษนี้ เป็นการแปลใหม่หมด มิได้ใช้วิธีคัดลอกจากที่ฝรั่งแปลไว้ แม้จะคัดลอกก็ทำไม่ได้สะดวก เพราะเป็นสุภาษิตที่คัดมาจากพระไตรปิฎกหลายเล่ม ไม่ใช่จากเรื่องใดเรื่องหนึ่งโดยเฉพาะ ฉะนั้น จึงถือได้ว่า เป็นงานริเริ่มของคนไทย ในการแปลภาษาบาลีเป็นอังกฤษ ซึ่งทางสภาการศึกษาจะได้ส่งเสริมให้มีการแปลมากขึ้นในโอกาสต่อไป.

ในที่นี้จะขอยกตัวอย่างบางบทที่ฝรั่งแปลไว้ มาเทียบกับฉบับที่แปลในหนังสือนี้ ฉบับที่ฝรั่งแปล ได้เลือกสำนวนของ F. Max Muller ในหนังสือ Sacred Books of the East เล่ม ๑๐.

ข้อ ๓๖

ฉบับ แมกซมึลเลอร์

"Not a mother, not a father will do so much, nor any other relatives; a well-directed mind will do us greater service."

ฉบับ ไทยแปล

"A well-directed mind makes a man better than his parents or relatives can do to him."

ข้อ ๑๕๕

ฉบับ แมกซมึลเลอร์

"Not in the sky, not in the midst of the sea, not if we enter into the cliffs of the mountians, is there known a spot in the whole world where death could not overcome (the mortal)."

ฉบับ ไทยแปล

"Not in the sky, nor in the middle of the sea, nor in a cave of a mountain can be found a place where a mortal cannot be overcome by death."

โดยเหตุที่การจัดพิมพ์และตรวจปรู๊ฟมีเวลาจำกัดมาก ความบกพร่องต่าง ๆ จึงอาจมีขึ้นได้ ซึ่งหวังว่าจะได้รับอภัย.

อนึ่ง ถ้าท่านผู้ใดพบข้อผิดพลาดหรือไม่เห็นด้วย จะกรุณาทักท้วงไป ก็จะขอรับไว้พิจารณาด้วยความยินดี และขอบพระคุณยิ่ง.

สุชีพ ปุญญานุภาพ

๗ เมษายน ๒๔๙๙

CONTENTS

BUDDHASĀSANASUBHĀSITA

SECTION II

1. ATTAVAGGA – SECTION OF SELF.

1. Attadatthaṃ paratthena
bahunāpi na hāpaye
attadatthamabhiññāya
sadatthapasuto siyā.

Let no man neglect his own profit (spiritual development) for the sake of others, however important they may be. Realizing what is for one's own profit, let him attend to it earnestly.

(This stanza was given by the Lord Buddha when groups of his disciples after learning from him that he would utterly pass away (parinibbāna) within three months gathered together consulting each other "what can we do, what can we do." They spent their times in this way neglecting their daily practice of concentration and meditation. When the Lord knew this he then warned them to attend to their daily practice for spiritual development.)

2. Attānañce tathā kayirā
yathaññamanusāsati
sudanto vata dametha
attā hi kira duddamo.

Behave yourself as you instruct others. Train yourself first before training others, for it is difficult to train one's own self.

3. **Attānameva paṭhamaṃ**
patirūpe nivesaye
athaññamanusāseyya
na kilisseyya paṇḍito.

Let a wise man establish himself on the proper Path first, then he may instruct others. Such a wise man should not blemish himself.

2. APPAMĀDAVAGGA—SECTION OF CARELESSNESS.

4. **Appamatto pamattesu**
suttesu bahujāgaro
abalassaṃva sīghasso
hitvā yāti sumedhaso.

Being watchful among careless persons, awake among those sleeping, the wise man advances like a strong horse, leaving behind him the weakling.

5. **Uṭṭhānavato satimato**
sucikammassa nisammakārino
saññatassa ca dhammajīvino
appamattassa yasobhivaddhati.

There is a steady increase in the reputation of him who is energetic, mindful, blameless in deeds, who is careful in his ations, and who is self-controlled, righteous in living and also earnest.

6. Mā pamādamanuyuñjetha
mā kāmaratisanthavaṃ
appamatto hi jhāyanto
pappoti paramaṃ sukhaṃ.

Never be endowed with carelessness Do not associate with sensuality. He who is watchful and has a concentrated mind will attain the highest bliss.

3. KAMMAVAGGA – SECTION OF ACTION.

7. Atisītaṃ atiuṇhaṃ
atisāyamidaṃ ahu
iti vissaṭṭhakammante
atthā accenti māṇave.

"Too cold, too hot, too late" can always be the excuses to those who do not want to work. They let their chance pass by.

8. Atha pāpāni kammāni
karaṃ bālo na bujjhati
sehi kammehi dummedho
aggidaḍḍhova tappati.

The wicked fool is unconscientious in his doing evil deeds. He will be tormented later on, as if being burnt, by the fruit of such evil deeds of his own.

9. Yādisaṃ vapate bījaṃ
tādisaṃ labhate phalaṃ
kalyāṇakārī kalyāṇaṃ
pāpakārī ca pāpakaṃ.

One reaps whatever one has sown. Those who do good receive good and those who do evil reveive evil.

10. Yo pubbe katakalyāṇo
katattho nāvabujjhati
atthā tassa palujjanti
ye honti abhipatthitā.

He who does not realize the benefit done to him destroys all goodness he wishes for.

11. Yo pubbe katakalyāṇo
katattho manubujjhati
atthā tassa pavaḍḍhanti
ye honti abhipatthitā.

He who realizes the benefit done to him will have all the goodness he wishes for.

12. Yo pubbe karaṇīyāni
pacchā so kātumicchati
varuṇakaṭṭhaṃ bhañjova
sa pacchā anutappati.

One who wants to do afterwards what should be done first, remorses like the youth (in a fable) who breaks (carelessly) the branches of the varuṇa tree.

13. Sace pubbe katahetu
sukhadukkhaṃ nigacchati
porāṇakaṃ kataṃ pāpaṃ
tameso muñcate iṇaṃ.

Happiness and suffering experienced through the previous accumulated Kammas (action) are like the settling of the old accounts wherein one has to pay for the balance.

14. Sukhakāmāni bhūtāni
yo daṇḍena vihiṃsati
attano sukhamesāno
pecca so na labhate sukhaṃ.

All sentient beings are seekers after happiness. He who, for the sake of his own happiness, violates other persons, will never attain happiness afterwards.

15. Sukhakāmāni bhūtāni
yo daṇḍena na hiṃsati
attano sukhamesāno
pecca so labhate sukhaṃ.

All sentient beings are seekers after happiness. He who does not violate other persons for the sake of his happiness will attain happiness afterwards.

4. KILESAVAGGA – SECTION OF PASSION.

16. Kāmā kaṭukā āsīvisūpamā
yesu mucchitā bālā
te dīgharattaṃ niraye
samappitā haññante dukkhitā.

Bitter and, poisonous as a serpent's poison, is sensual desire with which fools are infatuated. Crowded in hell, they have to spend their long, tortured lives there.

17. Kuhā thaddhā lapā siṃgī
unnaḷā cāsamāhitā
na te dhamme virūhanti
sammāsambuddhadesite.

Those who are deceitful, brusque, prone to babbling, tricky, insolent and have no self-control, cannot make any progress in following the Doctrine declared by the All-Enlightened One.

18. Kodhassa visamūlassa
madhuraggassa brāhmaṇa
vadhaṃ ariyā pasaṃsanti
tañhi chetvā na socati.

Anger has sweet tops born of poisoned roots. Blessed by the wise is he who, having killed that anger, never has to regret.

19. Niddaṃ na bahulīkareyya
jāgariyaṃ bhajeyya ātāpī
tandiṃ māyaṃ hasaṃ khiḍḍaṃ
methunaṃ vippajahe savibhūsaṃ.

Those who wish to burn up their passions must not indulge in sleeping, but must diligently associate themselves with watchfulness. They must also rid themselves of laziness, hypocrisy, merriment and all sensual pleasures together with their elements.

20. Paravajjānupassissa
niccaṃ ujjhānasaññino
āsavā tassa vaḍḍhanti
ārā so āsavakkhayā.

Latent passions always pile up in a fault-finder, who always complains of others' faults. Such a person is far from the extinction of his passions.

21. Yadā dvayesu dhammesu
pāragū hoti brāhmaṇo
athassa sabbe saṃyogā
atthaṃ gacchanti jānato.

Whenever a Noble One reaches the shore (destination) of the 2 kinds of phenomena (Mundane & Supra-mundane), all his binding ropes of passion come to an end.

22. Yā kācimā duggatiyo
asmiṃ loke paramhi ca
avijjāmūlakā sabbā
icchā lobhasamussayā.

Rooted in ignorance is suffering in the present life and in the hereafter which is framed up by desire and greed.

23. Yena sallena otiṇṇo
disā sabbā vidhāvati
tameva sallaṃ abbuyha
na dhāvati na sīdati.

He who is shot by an arrow (of passion) has to run in all directions. Having taken it out, he no more runs nor sinks.

24. Lobho doso ca moho ca
purisaṃ pāpacetasaṃ
hiṃsanti attasambhūtā
tacasāraṃva samphalaṃ.

Just as the bamboo is killed by its own fruit, so is a wicked person ruined by hatred, greed and delusion born of his own wicked mind.

5. KHANTIVAGGA — SECTION OF FORBEARANCE.

25. Attanopi paresañca
atthāvaho va khantiko
saggamokkhagamaṃ maggaṃ
āruḷho hoti khantiko.

He who has forbearance brings benefit to others as well as to himself. He is also treading on the path to heaven and to the extinction of passions.

26. Kevalānaṃpi pāpānaṃ
khantī mūlaṃ nikantati
garahakalahādīnaṃ
mūlaṃ khanati khantiko.

Forbearance eradicates all evils. He who is equipped with forbearance uproots the unpleasant causes such as blame and quarrel.

27. Khantiko mettavā lābhī
yasassī sukhasīlavā
piyo devamanussānaṃ
manāpo hoti khantiko.

He who is provided with forbearance and loving-kindness is always lucky, honoured and happy. He is also beloved and appreciated by divine and human beings.

28. Satthuno vacanovādaṃ
karotiyeva khantiko
paramāya ca pūjāya
jinaṃ pūjeti khantiko.

He who is endowed with forbearance is called the real follower of the Buddha. He is said to revere the Buddha with the highest kind of worship.

29. Sīlasamādhiguṇānaṃ
khantī padhānakāraṇaṃ
sabbepi kusalā dhammā
khantyāyeva vaḍḍhanti te.

Forbearance is the chief cause of all virtues such as morality and concentration All other virtues increase with the development of forbearance.

6. CITTAVAGGA – SECTION OF THE MIND.

30. Anavatṭhitacittassa
saddhammaṃ avijānato
paripalvapasādassa
paññā na paripūrati.

There is no perfection of the wisdom of one who has a fluctuating mind, does not know the good doctrine and has a shaking faith.

31. Appamāṇaṃ hitaṃ cittaṃ
paripuṇṇaṃ subhāvitaṃ
yaṃ pamāṇaṃ kataṃ kammaṃ
na taṃ tatrāvasissati.

A well-wishing mind which is well-trained, made unlimited and complete has no limited Karma (action) left.

32. Ânāpānassati yassa
aparipuṇṇā abhāvitā
kāyopi iñjito hoti
cittampi hoti iñjitaṃ.

Restless are the body and mind on him whose concentration on the breaths is not yet made complete and cultivated.

33. Ānāpānassati yassa
paripuṇṇā subhāvitā
kāyopi aniñjito hoti
cittampi hoti aniñjitaṃ.

Calm are the body and mind of him whose concentration on the breaths has been made complete and well-cultivated.

34. Diso disaṃ yantaṃ kayirā
verī va pana verinaṃ
micchāpaṇihitaṃ cittaṃ
pāpiyo naṃ tato kare.

A mis-directed mind causes a worse destruction than a robber or an enemy can do to each other.

35. Dūraṅgamaṃ ekacaraṃ
asarīraṃ guhāsayaṃ
ye cittaṃ saññamessanti
mokkhanti mārabandhanā.

Being formless and encased in the body, the mind is a far and lone wanderer. He who can put a curb on it will be free from the bonds of Māra (the Evil One)

36. Na tam mātā pitā kayirā
aññe vāpica ñātakā
sammāpaṇihitaṃ cittaṃ
seyyaso naṃ tato kare.

A well-directed mind makes a man better than his parents or relatives can do to him.

37. Phandanaṃ capalaṃ cittaṃ
durakkhaṃ dunnivārayaṃ
ujuṃ karoti medhāvī
usukārova tejanaṃ.

Always wavering and flitting, as well as unruly and stubborn is this mind. A wise man can still it just as a fletcher straightens his arrows.

38. Yathā agāraṃ ducchannaṃ
vutthi samativijjhati
evaṃ abhāvitaṃ cittaṃ
rāgo samativijjhati.

Just as rain leaks through an ill-thatched house, so lust leaks through an un-trained mind.

39. Yo ca saddaparittāsī
vane vātamigo yathā
lahucittoti taṃ āhu
nāssa sampajjate vataṃ.

He who is easily frightened at the sound like a jungle deer, is called the "light-minded". His ascetic observance is liable to failure.

40. Vārijo va thale khitto
okamokataubbhato
pariphandatidaṃ cittaṃ
māradheyyaṃ pahātave.

Like a fish taken out of its watery home and thrown onto the land, this mind, when parted with its haunts of sensual enjoyments in order to disregard Māra's influence, will give a desperate struggle.

41. Saññāya viparīyesā
cittante pariḍayhati
nimittaṃ parivajjehi
subhaṃ rāgūpasañhitaṃ.

Your mind is always consumed with your own misconception. Abstain from associating it with lustful influences.

42. Selo yathā ekaghano
vātena na samīrati
evaṃ nindāpasaṃsāsu
na samiñjanti paṇḍitā.

As a mountain of solid rock remains unshaken by the storm, so the wise man remains unmoved by praise or blame.

7. DĀNAVAGGA—SECTION OF CHARITY.

43. Aggasmiṃ dānaṃ dadataṃ
aggaṃ puññaṃ pavaḍḍhati
aggaṃ āyu ca vaṇṇo ca
yaso kitti sukhaṃ balaṃ

When one dispenses a charity to the excellent one, his excellent merit multiplies. So also are his age, complexion, rank, honour, happiness and strength.

44. Aggadāyī varadāyī
seṭṭhadāyī ca yo naro
dīghāyu yasavā hoti
yattha yatthūpapajjati.

In every birth he who gives out what is excellent, nicest and choicest will be endowed with long life and nobility.

45. Nīharetheva dānena
dinnaṃ hoti sunibbhataṃ
dinnaṃ sukhaphalaṃ hoti
nādinnaṃ hoti taṃ tathā.

(When the world is consumed by the fires of old age and death) Take out your (worldly) things by way of charity. Those given are safely taken out and result in happiness, while those not given are not so

46. Pubbe dānādikaṃ datvā
idānī labhatī sukhaṃ
mūleva siñcitaṃ hoti
agge ca phaladāyakaṃ.

Present happiness is the result of charity and other merits previously done. This can be seen in a tree which bears fruit at its top after the roots have been watered.

47. Yathā vārivahā pūrā
paripūrenti sāgaraṃ
evameva ito dinnaṃ
petānaṃ upakappati.

Just as an ocean is filled by great rivers which are full, the dedicated charity dispensed here is received by the deceased.

**48. So ca sabbadado hoti
yo dadāti upassayaṃ
amatandado ca so hoti
yo dhammamanusāsati.**

He gives all who gives a dwelling place. He gives Immorality who gives instructions of Righteousness.

8. DHAMMAVAGGA – SECTION OF RIGHTEOUSNESS.

**49. Adhammaṃ paṭipannassa
yo dhammamanusāsati
tassa ce vacanaṃ kayirā
na so gaccheyya duggatiṃ.**

An immoral person may not have a miserable existence, if, being instructed, he follows the law of Righteousnees.

**50. Upārambhacitto dummedho
suṇāti jinasāsanaṃ
ārakā hoti saddhammā
nabhā so paṭhavī yathā.**

Just as the earth is far from the sky, so is an ignorant and obstinate person from the good doctrine even though he may have listened to the Buddha's message.*

51. **Khattiyā brāhmaṇā vessā**
suddhā caṇḍālapukkusā
idha dhammaṃ caritvāna
bhavanti tidive samā.

Having lived up to the Doctrine, all are equal in heaven of the three devinities, no matter whether they are kings, brahmins, merchants, labourers, half-castes, or refuse-cleaners.

52. **Tanhādutiyo puriso**
dīghamaddhāna saṃsaraṃ
itthambhāvaññathābhāvaṃ
sansāraṃ nātivattati.

Long is the wandering over the states of being this and being that, when a person is befriended by craving. Never can he go beyond the cycle of rebirths.

53. **Nabhañca dūre pathavī ca dūre**
pāraṃ samuddassa tadāhu dūre
tato have dūrataraṃ vadanti
satañca dhammo asatañca rāja.

O Lord, far is the earth from the sky. Far are the shores of the ocean from each other. But much farther still, it is said, is the nature of the virtuous one from that of the wicked one

**54. Nikkuhā nillapā dhīrā
athaddhā susamāhitā
te ve dhamme virūhanti
sammāsambuddhadesite.**

Those who do not cheat nor is given to frivolous talk, who is wise, not brusque, and who is well-poised, will make rapid progress in the doctrine promulgated by the All-Enlighened One.

**55. Patisotagāmiṃ nipuṇaṃ
gambhīraṃ duddasaṃ aṇuṃ
rāgarattā na dakkhanti
tamokkhandhena āvutā.**

Beings are absorbed in the deepest dye of lust and wrapped up in the pitch-dark of ignorance. They do not realize the Buddha's doctrine which is against the strong current of passions, and which is delicate, profound, very difficult to understand, and subtle.

**56. Yadā ca buddhā lokasmiṃ
uppajjanti pabhaṅkarā
te imaṃ dhammaṃ pakāsenti
dukkhūpasamagāminaṃ**

With the advent of the Buddhas who are the torch-bearers, the doctrine leading to the extincion of suffering is thereby proclaimed.

57. Yassa sabrahmacārīsu
gāravo nūpalabbhati
ārakā hoti saddhammā
nabhaṃ pathaviyā yathā.

In whom there is no respect for other members of the Order, far from the Dhamma is he as far from the sky is the earth

58. Ye ca kho sammadakkhāte
dhamme dhammanuvattino
te janā pāramessanti
maccudheyyaṃ suduttaraṃ

Those who follow the well-preached doctrine of the Buddha will be able to cross over the sway of Death which is extremely difficult to go beyond and then reach the bank (of Nibbāna).

59. Yo icche dibbabhogañca
dibbamāyuṃ yasaṃ sukhaṃ
pāpāni parivajjetvā
tividhaṃ dhammamācare.

Those who wish for divine wealth, life, glory and happiness should avoid doing all kinds of evil and should also practise the three phases of Right Conduct (physical, verbal and mental).

60. Yo ca appampi sutvāna
dhammaṃ kāyena passati
sa ve dhammadharo hoti
yo dhammaṃ nappamajjati

One who has the intuitive experience of the Dhamma though he listens to it but little and who does not neglect it is the maintainer of the Dhamma.

61. Yoniso vicine dhamaṃ
paññāyatthaṃ vipassati
pajjotasseva nibbānaṃ
vimokkho hoti cetaso.

Consider the Dhamma wisely. Only through wisdom can the realization of its meaning be attained. Spiritual deliverance is just like the extinction of a flame.

9. PAKIṆṆAKAVAGGA–MISCELLANEOUS SECTION.

62. Akkocchi maṃ avadhi maṃ
ajini maṃ ahāsi me
ye ca taṃ upanayhanti
veraṃ tesaṃ na sammati.

"He insulted me, injured me, defeated me, robbed me." In those who harbour such thoughts hatred never ceases.

63. Akkocchi maṃ avadhi maṃ
ajini maṃ ahāsi me
ye ca taṃ nūpanayhanti
veraṃ tesūpasammati.

"He insulted me, injured me, defeated me, robbed me." In those who do not harbour such thoughts hatred does cease.

64. Acci yathā vātavegena khittaṃ
atthaṃ paleti na upeti saṃkhaṃ
evaṃ muni nāmakāyā vimutto
atthaṃ paleti na upeti saṁkhaṃ.

Just as a flame blown out by the wind is extinct and can never be described, so also is the Sage who is absolutely released from the mental compound.

65. Indriyāni manussānaṃ
hitāya ahitāya ca
arakkhitāni ahitāni
rakkhitāni hitāya ca.

Human sense-organs can be either useful or useless. Those uncontroled are useless while those controled are useful.

66. Tasmā hi paṇḍito poso
sampassaṃ atthamattano
lobhassa na vasaṃ gacche
haneyya disakaṃ manaṃ.

Discerning people, for the sake of their own benefit, should not allow themselves to be overpowered by covetousness. They should try to get rid of it.

67. Nakkhattaṃ patimānentaṃ
attho bhalaṃ upaccagā
attho atthassa nakkhattaṃ
kiṃ karissanti tārakā.

A chance always passes the fool who is calculating the position of stars. It is an auspicions occasion in itself. What can the stars do ?

68. Na sathu balavā balo
sāhasaṃ vindate dhanaṃ
kandantametaṃ dummedhaṃ
kaḍḍhanti nirayaṃ bhusaṃ

Baleful is the result when an influential villain takes a short-cut road to richness To the terrible realm of woe will the Lord of Hell drag down such a wailing fool.

69. Pañca kāmaguṇā loke
manochaṭṭhā paveditā
ettha chandaṃ virājitvā
evaṃ dukkhā pamuccati.

The five objects of sense-organs, with the mind as the sixth, were already made known. Whoever releases himself from sensual enjoyments will accordingly be liberated from suffering.

70. Paradukkhūpadhānena
yo attano sukhamicchati
verasaṃsaggasaṃsaṭṭho
verā so na parimuccati.

Those who seek for their happiness by harming or inflicting pain upon others are inextricably involved in hatred. They cannot be free from enmity.

71. Parittaṃ dārumāruyha
yathā sīde mahaṇṇave.
evaṃ kusītamāgamma
sādhujīvīpi sīdati.

Even as a person who clings to a scrap of wood in an ocean is sure to be drowned, so is a luxurious but lazy persondoomed to misery.

72. Balaṃ cando balaṃ suriyo
balaṃ samaṇabrāhmaṇā
balaṃ velā samuddassa
bhalātibalamitthiyo.

Great is the power of the moon, the sun, the hermit and the sea-shore. But greater still is that of a woman.

73. Bahūnaṃ vata atthāya
uppajjanti tathāgatā
itthīnaṃ purisānañca
ye te sāsanakārakā.

The Buddha's birth was for the benefit of the many. women as well as men, who follow his Doctrine.

74. Yattha posaṃ na jānanti
jātiyā vinayena vā
na tattha mānaṃ kayirātha
vasaṃ aññātake jane.

You cannot expect people to give you due respect when you are in a place where your birth and qualifications are not yet recognized.

75. Ye ca kāhanti ovādaṃ
nara buddhena desitaṃ
sotthipāraṃ gamissanti
valāheneva vānijā.

Those who follow the Buddha's teachings will reach the bank of safety as the merchants reach their destination safely with the help of their horse named Valāhaka.

76. Ye vuḍḍhamapacāyanti
narā dhammasa kovidā
ditthe dhamme ca pāsaṃsā
samparāyo ca suggati.

Those who are wise in the Dhamma and who revere their superiors are praised in their present lives and are are also blessed with happy lives hereafter.

77. Rūpā saddā gandhā rasā
phassā dhammā ca kevalā
etaṃ lokāmisaṃ ghoraṃ
ettha loko vimucchito.

All the- sight, sound, smell, taste, touch and the mental phenomena - are terrible worldly temptations into which beings are deeply merged.

78. Videsavāsaṃ vasato
jātavedasamenapi
khamitabbaṃ sapaññena
api dāsassa tajjitaṃ.

It is advisable for a wise person staying in a foreign land, however brilliant as a fire he is, to endure the threatening even of the (native) slave.

10. PAÑÑĀVAGGA – SECTION OF WISDOM

79. Appassutāyaṃ puriso
balivaddova jīrati
maṃsāni tassa vaḍḍhanti
paññā tassa na vaḍḍhati.

The uneducated, like an old bull, gradually fade away. Their flesh increases but not their wisdom.

80. Jīvatevapi sappañño
api vittaparikkhayā
paññāya ca alābhena
vittavāpi na jīvati.

A wise man can manage (his life) even though he lacks wealth. But lacking wisdom, no fool can hold his ground.

81. Paññavā buddhisampanno
vidhānavidhikovido
kālaññū samayaññū ca
sa rājavasatiṃ vase.

An intelligent person, with the gift of discernment, knowing how to manage affairs, and clever at (selecting) the proper time and season, can be in the government service.

82. Paññā hi setthā kusalā vadanti
nakkhattarājāriva tārakānaṃ
sīlaṃ sirī cāpi satañca dhammo
anvāyikā paññavato bhavanti.

Wisdom, say the intelligent persons, is the best, as is the moon among all the stars. Discipline, glory and other virtuous natures follow the wise man.

83. Mattāsukhapariccāgā
passe ce vipulaṃ sukhaṃ
caje mattāsukhaṃ dhīro
sampassaṃ vipulaṃ sukaṃ.

Seeing that perfect happiness can be attained by sacrificing the inferior one, a wise man should abandon it for the sake of the perfect one.

**84. Yasaṃ laddhāna dummedho
anatthaṃ carati attano
attano ca paresañca
hiṃsāya paṭipajjati.**

Having obtained power, a fool (usually) corrupts himself, and so hurts himself as well as others through his action.

**85. Yāvadeva anatthāya
ñattaṃ bālassa jāyati
hanti bālassa sukkaṃsaṃ
muddhaṃ assa vipātayaṃ.**

A villain's cleverness is only for his own destruction. It corrupts his brains and kills his virtuous nature.

**86. Yo ca vassasataṃ jīve
duppañño asamāhito
ekāhaṃ jīvitaṃ seyyo
paññavantassa jhāyino.**

A hundred years' living of an ignorant, wavering person is not worth one day of a wise man whose mind is concentrated.

11. PAMĀDAVAGGA – SECTION OF CARELESSNESS.

87. Bahumpi ce sahitaṃ bhāsamāno
na takkaro hoti naro pamatto
gopova gāvo gaṇayaṃ paresaṃ
na bhāgavā sāmaññassa hoti.

A careless person talking the Buddha's words without putting any of them to practice himself, is like a hired cowboy counting the cows for others (never tasting their milk or having a part of the sale). Such a person can never share the taste of the four Stages of the Path.

88. Yañhi kiccaṃ tadapaviddhaṃ
akiccaṃ pana kayīrati
unnalānaṃ pamattānaṃ
tesaṃ vaḍḍhanti āsavā.

Passions increase in those haughty, careless persons who ignore what has to be done first and take up what ought to be done afterwards.

89. Yo ca pubbe pamajjitvā
pacchā so nappamajjati
somaṃ lokaṃ pabhāseti
abbhā muttova candimā.

He glorifies the world who was formerly careless but has afterwards become mindful. Such a person is like the moon emerging from the clouds.

12. PĀPAVAGGA — SECTION OF SIN

90. Idha socati pecca socati
pāpakārī ubhayattha socati
so socati so vihaññati
disvā kammakiliṭṭhamattano.

A sinful person, having come to realize his evil deeds, has to experience a twofold regret i.e. in this present life and in the hereafter.

91. Udabindunipātena
udakumbhopi pūrati
āpūrati bālo pāpassa
thokaṃ thokaṃpi ācinaṃ.

Even as a water-pot can be filled by the dripping of water, so a villain can be filled by his gradually accumulated evils.

92. Ekaṃ dhammaṃ atītassa
musāvādissa jantuno
vitiṇṇaparalokassa
natthi pāpaṃ akāriyaṃ.

There is no sin which is so great that a liar cannot do, since he has put aside one virtue (of honesty) anp ignores (the just retribution in) the hereafter.

93. Na hi pāpaṃ kataṃ kammaṃ
sajjukhīraṃva muccati
ḍahantaṃ bālamanveti
bhasmācchannova pāvako.

Evil, like milk freshly obtained during the day, does not undergo a change. Its burning effect, however, (potentially) follows the evil-doer like a fire covered with ashes.

94. Pāṇimhi ce vaṇo nāssa
hareyya pāṇinā visaṃ
nābbaṇaṃ visamanveti
natthi pāpaṃ akubbato.

He whose hand is not wounded can carry poison. A poisonous liquid cannot seep into such a hand, nor can evil befall him who has done no wrong.

95. Yo ca sameti pāpāni
aṇuṃthūlāni sabbaso
samitattā hi pāpānaṃ
samaṇoti pavuccati.

One who has calmed down all kinds of evil, small and great, is called a "Samaṇa". — one who calms down evils.

96. Vānijova bhayaṃ maggaṃ
appasattho mahaddhano
visaṃ jīvitukāmova
pāpāni parivajjaye.

Let a man avoid evil as does a merchant, having (only) few companions (but) possessing great wealth, avoid a dangerous road, or as does a person, still clinging to life, avoid a poison.

13. PUGGALAVAGGA – SECTION OF MAN

97. Accayaṃ desayantīnaṃ
yo ce na paṭiganhati
kopantaro dosagaru
sa veraṃ paṭimuccati.

One who is given to anger and ill-will thereby refusing to forgive others' faults, which have been confessed, heaps hatred upon himself.

98. Appakā te manussesu
ye janā pāragāmino
athāyaṃ itarā pajā
tīramevānudhāvati.

Of all men, very few can cross the stream of life and death to the other bank of safety (Nibbāna). The rest of them only run up and down on this side of the bank (of life and death).

99. Asubhāya cittaṃ bhāvehi
ekaggaṃ susamāhitaṃ
sati kāyagatā tyatthu
nibbidābahulo bhava.

'Train your mind to be well-poised with the contemplation of the impurities of the body. Fix your attention on the body. Safeguard your weariness of worldly life.

100. Ahiṃsakā ye munayo
niccaṃ kāyena saṃvutā
te yanti accutaṃ ṭhānaṃ
yattha gantvā na socare.

Those Sages who practise the virtue of non-violence and who are always self-restrained, will attain the everlasting state where they will be perfectly free from sorrow.

101. Evaṃ kicchābhato poso
pitu aparicārako
pitari micchācaritvāna
nirayaṃ so upapajjati.

He who was brought up with difficulty by his parents but does not minister to their wants and behave wrongly towards them, is doomed to enter the realm of misery

102. Evaṃ buddhaṃ sarantānaṃ
dhammaṃ saṅghañca bhikkhavo
bhayaṃ vā chambhitattaṃ vā
lomahaṃso na hessati.

O Bhikkhus, while you are thus recollectring the Buddha (the Enlightened One), the Dhamma (the Law) and the Sangha (the Order), you will be free from fear, fright, and also from being startled.

103. Evaṃ mandassa posassa
bālassa avijānato
sārambhā jāyate kodho
sopi teneva dayhati.

A fool, misled by his own folly, is often burnt by his own anger because of his showing off with malicious intention

104. Onodaro yo sahate jighacchaṃ
danto tapassī mitapānabhojano
āhārahetu na karoti pāpaṃ
taṃ ve naraṃ samanamāhu loke.

He is called a "Samaṇa" (one who has calmed down his mind) who is not overpowered by hunger even though he is hungry, who is self-controlled, equipped with perseverance, moderate in his food and drink, and never commits a sin for the sake of (obtaining) food.

105. Kāme giddhā kāmaratā
kāmesu adhimucchitā
narā pāpāni katvāna
upapajjanti duggatiṃ.

He is doomed to enter the Realm of Misery who, being absorbed in and delighted with sensual pleasure, is deeply merged in it and commits a sin (for its sake).

106. Gāme vā yadivāraññe
ninne vā yadivā thale
yattha arahanto viharanti
taṃ bhūmirāmaṇeyyakaṃ.

The living-place of an Arahat (Worthy One), be it a village or a forest, in the low land or on the plateau, is always delightful.

107. Coditā devadūtehi
ye pamajjanti māṇavā
te dīgharattaṃ socanti
hīnakāyūpagā narā.

Warned by the Divine Messengers, those who are still careless will enter the lower existence and regret for a long time

108. Coro yathā sandhimukhe gahito
sakammunā haññati pāpadhammo
evaṃ pajā pecca paramhi loke
sakammunā haññati pāpadhammo.

Just as the vicious robber is caught at the opening (made by himself for the purpose of entering the house with a thieving intention) and will have to regret his own crime, so in the hereafter will the persons who have committed a sin.

109. Jātithaddho dhanathaddho
gottathaddho ca yo naro
saññātiṃ atimaññeti
taṃ parābhavato mukhaṃ.

It is a cause of ruin to be proud of one's birth, wealth and family name and then to despise even one's own relatives.

110. Taṃ brūmi upasantoti
kāmesu anapekkhinaṃ
ganthā tassa na vijjanti
atāri so visattikaṃ.

He is called "One who has attained perfect Tranquility" who is indifferent to sensual pleasure, has no binding rope of passion and has overcome his craving which is the great cause of restlessness.

111. Tejavāpi hi naro vicakkhaṇo
sakkato bahujanassa pūjito
nārīnaṃ vasaṅgato na bhāsati
rāhunā upahatova candimā.

An eclipsed moon enjoys no brightness or splendour, nor does a man who is under a woman's influence, even though he may be influential, wise, respected and worshipped by the public.

112. Dūre santo pakāsenti
himavantova pabbato
asantettha na dissanti
rattiṃ khittā yathā sarā.

The virtuous, like the Himalayas, appear from far away, while the vicious, like an arrow shot into the dark of the night, always disappears.

113. Dhīro bhoge adhigamma
saṅgaṇhāti ca ñātake
tena so kittiṃ pappoti
pecca sagge pamodati.

A wise man, having obtained wealth, ussually helps his relatives. He is accordingly beloved here and will also rejoice in the hereafter.

114. Na paṇḍitā attasukhassa hetu
pāpāni kammāni samācaranti
dukkhena phuṭṭhā khalitāpi santā
chandā ca dosā na jahanti dhammaṃ.

Never deos a wise man commit a sin for the sake of his happiness. Never will he discard Morality because of his personal love or hatred, even though he may suffer and meet with a failure.

115. Na ve anatthakusalena
atthacariyā sukhāvahā
hāpeti atthaṃ dummedho
kapi ārāmiko yathā.

To do good without knowing (what is) good never brings about happiness. The fool, like a monkey taking care of the orchard, destroys his own benefit.

116. Na hi sabbesu ṭhānesu
puriso hoti paṇḍito
itthīpi paṇḍitā hoti
tattha tattha vicakkhaṇā.

Not only can a man be called "wise," but also can a woman who is endowed with wisdom be so called.

117. Nindāya nappavedheyya
na uṇṇameyya pasaṃsito bhikkhu
lobhaṃ saha macchariyena
kodhaṃ pesuṇiyañca panudeyya.

A Bhikkhu must not shrink because of blame nor swell because of praise. He must try to get rid of his covetousness, miserliness, anger and slander.

118. Paṇḍito ca viyatto ca
vibhāvī ca vicakkhaṇo
khippaṃ moceti attānaṃ
mā bhāyitthāgamissati.

He who is wise, sensible, has a clear understanding, and is quick-witted, can suddenly free himself (from suffering). Do not be afraid. He will come back.

119. Paṇḍitoti samaññāto
ekacariyaṃ adhiṭṭhito
yathāpi methune yutto
mando va parikissati.

He is wise who purposely remains single, whereas he stains himself who is addicted to sexual intercourse.

120. Pahāya pañcāvaraṇāni cetaso
upakkilese byāpanujja sabbe
anissito chetvā sinehadosaṃ
eko care khaggavisāṇakappo.

He has abandoned the five mental hindrances and has destroyed his mental impurities. Having done away with his love and hatred, he is not possessed by thirst and wrong views. Such a person generally wanders alone like the rhinoceros's horn.

121. Puttā matthi dhanamatthi
iti bālo vihaññati
attā hi attano natthi
kuto puttā kuto dhanaṃ.

A fool suffers because he thinks that he has children, and he possesses wealth. Since he himself is not his own, how can a "son" or "wealth" belong to him?

122. Brahmāti mātāpitaro
pubbācariyāti vuccare
āhuneyyā ca puttānaṃ
pajāya anukampakā.

Parents are the supreme gods to their children. They are also called the children's first teachers. They are their greatest objects of worship and the patrons of beings.

123. Madhuvā maññatī bālo
yāva pāpaṃ na paccati
yadā ca paccatī pāpaṃ
atha dukkhaṃ nigacchati.

As long as an evil does not bear fruit, so long will the fool imagine it as sweet. But when it bears fruit, he will then experience suffering

124. Yaṃ ussukkā saṅgharanti
alakkhikā bahuṃ dhanaṃ
sippavanto asippā vā
lakkhikā tāni bhuñjare.

An ill-fated person may accumulate wealth, but a (more) fortunate person, whether skilful or not, will come to use it (will benefit by it).

125. Yaṃ yaṃ janapadaṃ yāti
nigame rājadhāniyo
sabbattha pūjito hoti
yo mittānaṃ na dubbhati.

He is respected wherever he goes, be it a town or a city, because he does not betray his friends.

126. Yato ca hoti pāpiccho
ahiriko anādayo
tato pāpaṃ pasavati
apāyaṃ tena gacchati.

Since he has evil desire, does not listen to his own conscience nor pay attention to the doctrine, he will have to face sin and thereby enter the lower plane of existence.

127. Yamhā dhammaṃ vijāneyya
sammāsambuddhadesitaṃ
sakkaccaṃ naṃ namasseyya
aggihuttaṃva brāhmaṇo.

Just as the brahmins worship the fire, so should you worship him by whom the doctrine, well-preached by the All-Enlightened one, is made known to you.

128. Yassa papaṃ kataṃ kammaṃ
kusalena pithīyati
somaṃ lokaṃ pabhāseti
abbhā muttova candimā.

Just as the moon merging from the clouds does brilliantly shine, so does a person by doing good leave his past evils behind.

129. Yassa rukkhassa chāyāya
nisīdeyya sayeyya vā
na tassa sākhaṃ bhañjeyya
mittadubbho hi pāpako.

He should not break the branches of a tree under whose shade he used to sleep or sit, for a wicked man is he who betrays his friend.

130. Ye ca dhammassa kusalā
porāṇassa disampati
carittena ca sampannā
na te gacchanti duggatiṃ.

O Your Majesty! He who is wise in the ancient law of Righteousness and is well-behaved will never go to the lower state of existence.

131. Ye na kāhanti ovādaṃ
narā buddhena desitaṃ
byasanaṃ te gamissanti
rakkhasīhiva vāṇijā.

Just as the merchants meet with disaster because of the water-demon, so will those who do not follow the instructions given by the Enlightened One.

132. Yo cattānaṃ samukkaṃse
pare ca avajānati
nihīno sena mānena
taṃ jaññā vasalo iti.

He who is self-extolling and treats other with contempt, degrades himself through his own conceit. He should be known as a wretch.

133. Yo ca sīlañcā paññañca
sutañcattani passati
ubhinnamatthaṃ carati
attano ca parassa ca.

Endowed with morality, wisdom and learning, a man usually behaves for others' welfare as well as for himself.

134. Yo ca mettaṃ bhāvayati
appamānaṃ patissato
tanū saṃyojanā honti
passato upadhikkhayaṃ.

He who is equipped with mindfulness and who extends unlimited loving-kindness to all beings has destroyed his passions. His fetters are loosened.

135. Yo dandhakāle tarati
taranīye ca dandhaye
ayoniso saṃvidhānena
bālo dukkhaṃ nigacchati.

A fool has to suffer through his unwise management because he hurries when it is time to slow down but slows down when it is time to hurry.

136. Yo dandhakāle dandheti
taranīye ca tāraye
yoniso saṃvidhānena
sukhaṃ pappoti paṇḍito.

A wise man is happy because of his wise management knowing how to hurry when it is time to hurry and slow down when it is time to slow down.

137. Yo na hanti na ghāteti
na jināti na jāpaye
mettaso sabbabhūtānaṃ
verantassa na kenaci.

He who neither kills nor gives the order to kill and neither conquers nor gives the order to conquer cultivates his loving-kindness to all beings, thereby being at enmity with nobody.

138. Yo mātaraṃ pitaraṃ vā
macco dhammena posati
idheva naṃ pasaṃsanti
pecca sagge pamodati.

He who duly supports his parents is always praised in this very life. He will also rejoice in the hereafter.

139. Yo ve kataññū katavedi dhīro
kalyāṇamitto daḷhabhatti ca hoti
dukkhitassa sakkacca karoti kiccaṃ
tathāvidhaṃ sappurisaṃ vadanti.

A wise man who is grateful, faithfully keeps good company and duly gives a helping hand to those who are in trouble is called a virtuous person.

140. Yo have iṇamādāya
bhuñjamāno palāyati
na hi te iṇamatthīti
taṃ jaññā vasalo iti.

He should be known as a wretch who, after borrowing and spending other's money, runs away or refuses the debt.

141. Yo hoti byatto ca visārado ca
bahussuto dhammadharo ca hoti
dhammassa hoti anudhammacārī
sa tādiso vuccati saṅghasobhano.

He glorifies his group who is wise, courageous, learned, virtuous and lives up to the law of Righteousness.

142. Rāgañca dosañca pahāya moham
sandālayitvā saññojanāni
asantasaṃ jīvitasaṅkhayamhi
eko care khaggavisanakappo.

Having done away with lust, hatred and delusion together with all other fetters, he has no fear of death and wanders alone like a rhinoceros's horn.

143. Sace indriyasampanno
santo santipade rato
dhāreti antimaṃ dehaṃ
jetvā māraṃ savāhanaṃ.

He who has conquered Māra the Evil One together with his army has the last birth because he has perfected his mental forces, calmed down his mind and put it to rest.

144. Sace bhāyatha dukkhassa
sace vo dukkhamappiyaṃ
mākattha pāpakaṃ kammaṃ
āvī vā yadivā raho.

Being afraid of suffering and loathing it, you shoulp do no evil, both in the open and in the secret place.

145. Sabbā disā anuparigamma cetasā
nevajjhagā piyataramattanā kvaci
evaṃ piyo puthu attā paresaṃ
tasmā na hiṃse paramattakāmo.

I have sought through all directions for one whom I can love more than myself, but in vain. So also does everybody love himself most. Every self-lover should therefore not violate others.

146. Salābhaṃ nātimaññeyya
nāññesaṃ pihayañcare
aññesaṃ pihayaṃ bhikkhu
samādhiṃ nādhigacchati.

Let a man not look down upon his gains. Let him not crave for others'. A Bhikkhu, being greedy for others' gains, will never have a concentrated mind.

147. Sātiyesu anassāvī
atimāne ca no yuto
saṇho ca paṭibhāṇavā
na saddho na virajjati.

He is neither absorbed in sensual pleasure nor treat others with contempt. He also is gentle and ready-witted. Such a person is not credulous nor fluctuating.

148. Sarattā kāmabhogesu
giddhā kāmesu mucchitā
atisāraṃ na bujjhanti
macchā khippaṃva odditaṃ.

Those who are impassioned in sensual enjoyments, who are attached to and merged in sensuality, do not know of their overstepping, just as the fishes (not knowing their overstepping) suddenly enter into a trap.

149. Supinena yathāpi sangataṃ
patibuddho puriso na passati
evampi piyāyitāṃ janaṃ
petaṃ kālakataṃ na passati.

As an awaken' man does not see what he saw in who his dream, so a living man cannot see the deceased who were his beloved ones.

150. Sehi dārehi asantuṭṭho
vesiyāsu padussati
dussati paradāresu
taṃ parābhavato mukhaṃ.

He, who is not content with his own wife, who has an intercourse with prostitutes and goes to others' wives is doomed to destruction.

14. PUÑÑAVAGGA – SECTION OF MERIT

151. Idha nandati pecca nandati
katapuñño ubhayattha nandati
puññaṃ me katanti nandati
bhiyyo nandati sugatiṃ gato.

He who has done meritorious deeds rejoices both in his present life and in the hereafter. In his present life he rejoices that he has done good deeds. In the hereafter he will rejoice all the more

152. Idha modati pecca modati
katapuñño ubhayattha modati
so modati so pamodati
disvā kammavisuddhimattano.

He who has done meritorious deeds rejoices both in his present life and in the hereafter. Seeing the flawlessness of his actions, he rejoices more and more.

153. Puññañce puriso kayirā
kayirāthenaṃ punappunaṃ
tamhi chandhaṃ kayirātha
sukho puññassa uccayo.

If a man wants to do good, let him do it again and be glad of it, for happiness is the outcome of the accumulation of good deeds.

154. Māvamaññetha puññassa
na mattaṃ āgamissati
udabindunipātena
udakumbhopi pūrati
āpūrati dhīro puññassa
thokaṃ thokampi ācinaṃ.

Let a man not look down upon a small amount of good deeds, thinking that is will not bear fruit. This can be represented as a water-pot which can be filled by the dripping of water. A wise man, gradually accumulating his merits, will at length attain its perfection.

155. Sahāyo atthajātassa
hoti mittaṃ punappunaṃ
sayaṃ katāni puññāni
taṃ mittaṃ samparāyikaṃ.

Just as a companion (one who does not desert his friend) becomes a real friend of him who is in need of help, so is the accumulated merit to the person in the hereafter.

15. MACCUVAGGA — SECTION OF DEATH.

156. Accayanti ahorattā
jīvitaṃ uparujjhati
āyu khīyati maccānaṃ
kunnadīnaṃva odakaṃ.

Time flits by—day after day and night after night. The span of life is incessantly consumed. Life is gradually using up its duration like a rivulet being gradually dried up.

157. Appamāyu manussānaṃ
hīḷeyya naṃ suporiso
careyyādittasīsova
natthi maccussa nāgamo.

So short is human life that it should be treated by a virtuous person as a worthless thing. Since death is absolutely certain to come, let a man make haste (in putting the doctrine to practice) like a person whose head is already on fire.

158. Daharā ca mahantā ca
ye bālā ye ca panditā
sabbe maccuvasaṃ yanti
sabbe maccuparāyanā.

All sentient beings, whether young or old, foolish or wise, are to go to the power of death, which is their destination.

159. Na antalikkhe na samuddamajjhe
na pabbatānaṃ vivaraṃ pavīsaṃ
na vijjatī so jagatippadeso
yatraṭṭhitaṃ nappasaheyya maccu.

Not in the sky, nor in the middle of the sea, nor in cave of a mountain can be found a place where a mortal cannot be overcome by death.

160. Pupphāni heva pacinantaṃ
byāsattamanasaṃ naraṃ
atittaṃ yeva kāmesu
antako kurute vasaṃ.

Still busy gathering the attractive flowes of sensual pleasure, a man, imprisoned in the cocoon of sensuality will be caught up by death before he is satisfied.

161. Yathā daṇḍena gopālo
gāvo pājeti gocaraṃ
evaṃ jarā ca maccu ca
āyuṃ pājenti pāṇinaṃ.

Just as a cowherd drives out his cattle to pasture with a stave, so do old age and death drive out the life of man.

162. Yathāpi kumbhakārassa
katā mattikabhajanā
sabbe bhédapariyantā
evaṃ maccāna jīvitaṃ.

Just as clay-pots made by potters are to be broken at last, so are the lives of sentient beings.

163. Yathā vārivaho pūro
vahe rukkhe pakūlaje
evaṃ jarāya maranena
vuyhante sabbapāṇino.

Just as a flood sweeps away with its current the trees on either bank, so are the lives of sentient beings swept away by decay and death.

16. VĀCĀVAGGA – SECTION OF SPEECH

164. Kalyānimeva muñceyya
na hi muñceyya pāpikaṃ
mokkho kalyāniyā sādhu
mutvā tappati pāpikaṃ.

Only good words should be spoken, never evil ones. Uttering good words is profitable. One who utters evil words will have to regret.

165. Tameva vācaṃ bhāseyya
yāyattānaṃ na tāpaye
pare ca na vihiṃseyya
sā ve vācā subhāsitā.

One should speak a word which does not cause regret to himself and is not harmful to others. That kind of words is well-spoken.

166. Nātivelaṃ pabhāseyya
na tuṇhī sabbadā siyā
avikiṇṇaṃ mitaṃ vācaṃ
patte kāle udīraye.

One should not speak too much nor keep quiet all the time. When it is time to speak, let him speak moderately and not redundantly.

167. Piyavācameva bhāseyya
yā vācā paṭinanditā
yaṃ anādāya pāpāni
paresaṃ bhāsate piyaṃ.

Let a man speak what is pleasant and cheerful. A wise man does not pay attention to others' insult and always speak what is delightful.

168. Purisassa hi jātassa
kuthārī jāyate mukhe
yāya chindati attānaṃ
bālo dubbhāsitaṃ bhaṇaṃ.

An axe is born in a mouth of everyone. It is the axe with which a fool who says evil words wounds himself.

169. Yañhi kayirā tañhi vade
yaṃ na kayirā na taṃ vade
akarontaṃ bhāsamānaṃ
parijānanti paṇḍitā.

Let a man talk of what he can do, not of what he still cannot do. He who is merely clever at speaking, but not doing, will be detected by the wise man.

170. Yo attahetu parahetu
dhanahetu ca yo naro
sakkhiputtho musā brūti
taṃ jaññā vasalo iti.

He is a vicious person who gives false witness either for his own sake or for others' or for wealth.

171. Yo nindiyaṃ pasaṃsati
tam vā nindati yo pasaṃsiyo
viciṇāti mukhenaso kaliṃ
kalinā tena sukhaṃ na vindati.

He 'collects evil with his own mouth' when he praises one who should be blamed or blames one who should be praised Such a person will thereby never find happiness.

172. Sahassamapi ce vācā
anatthapadasañhitā
ekaṃ atthapadaṃ seyyo.
yaṃ sutvā upasammati.

A thousand useless words is not worth one by which the mind can be calmed after listening to it.

17. VIRIYAVAGGA – SECTION OF EFFORT.

173. Appakenapi medhāvī
pābhatena vicakkhaṇo
samuṭṭhāpeti attānaṃ
aṇuṃ aggiṃva sandhamaṃ

Just as a man blows a small fire into a flame, so a man of wisdom and discernment can make money even from a small investment.

8

**174. Amoghaṃ divasaṃ kayira
appena bahukena vā
yaṃ yaṃ vivahate ratti
tadūnantassa jīvitaṃ**

Let not a man waste his day and night from more on less benefit. The more he wastes, the more his life meets with emptiness.

**175. Utthātā kammadheyyesu
appamatto vidhānavā
samaṃ kappeti jīvitaṃ
sambhataṃ anurakkhati.**

He can safeguard his wealth who is industrious, careful, clever at managing the affairs and moderate in his mode of living.

**176. Cakkhumā visamānīva
vijjamāne parakkame
paṇḍito jīvalokasmiṃ
pāpāni parivajjaye.**

Let a man with perseverance abstain from doing evil deeds, like person who, not being blind, avoids the uneven roads.

177. Yo ca vassasataṃ jīve
kusīto hīnavīriyo
ekāhaṃ jīvitaṃ seyyo
viriyaṃ ārabhato dalhaṃ

A hundred years of a person who is lazy and inactive is not worth one day of him who has a strong effort.

178. Yo ca sītañca uṇhañca
tinā bhiyyo na maññati
karaṃ purisakiccāni
so sukhā na vihāyati.

When a man does not reckon the heat and cold more than the grass (does), he is sure to be rewarded with happiness in the long run.

18. SADDHĀVAGGA – SECTION OF FAITH.

179. Ekopi saddho medhāvī
assaddhānaṃ ca ñātinaṃ
dhammaṭṭho sīlasampanno
hoti atthāya bandhunaṃ.

Even though there may be one person in a family who has a reasonable faith, who is wise, righteous and well-behaved, that person can be helpful to his relatives or friends who have wrong views.

180. Dassanakāmo sīlavataṃ
saddhammaṃ sotumicchati
vineyya maccheramalaṃ
sa ve saddhoti vuccati.

He is called "Faithful" who wants to see the righteous one and listen to his teachings and who gets rid of his mental stain of miserliness.

181. Saddho sīlena sampanno
yaso bhogasamappito
yaṃ yaṃ padesaṃ bhajati
tattha tattheva pūjito.

He who has a reasonable faith, practises the Code of Discipline and Morality, and is endowed with wealth and rank, is always respected wherever he goes.

182. Ye naṃ dadanti saddāya
vippasannena cetasā
tameva annaṃ bhajati
asmiṃ loke paramhi ca.

Those who, out of piety and purity of mind, distribute rice, will obtain rice both in this world and in the hereafter.

19. SĪLAVAGGA – SECTION OF MORALITY.

183. Ādi sīlaṃ patiṭṭhā ca
kalyāṇānañca mātukaṃ
pamukhaṃ sabbadhammānaṃ
tasmā sīlaṃ visodhaye.

Precept is the first refuge, the source and the chief of all other virtues. Therefore let it be purified.

184. Avannañca akittiñca
dussīlo labhate naro
vaṇṇaṃ kittiṃ pasaṃsañca
sadā labhati sīlavā.

An immoral person usually heaps blame and disgrace upon himself, while one who acts in accordance with the law of morality will always receive admiration and respect.

185. Idheva kittiṃ labhati
pecca sagge ca sumano
sabbattha sumano dhīro
sīlesu susamāhito.

In his present life a wise man who is perfectly equipped with morality is always honoured. After his death he will enter into the realm of bliss. He is thus blessed with rejoice everywhere

186. Itheva nindaṃ labhati
peccāpāye ca dummano
sabbattha dummano bālo
sīlesu asamāhito.

A fool who is fickle in his practising morality is always blamed. He will even regret after his death. He is always doomed to misery.

187. Kāyena vacāya ca yodha saññato
manasā ca kiñci naroti pāpaṃ
na attahetu alikaṃ bhanāti
tathāvidhaṃ silavantaṃ vadanti.

He has his words, deeds and thoughts well-controled He never commits a sin nor talks non-sense for his own sake. Such a person is called "one who is endowed with morality."

188. Tasmā hi nārī ca naro ca sīlavā
atthaṅgupetaṃ upavassuposathaṃ
puññāni katvāna sukhudrayāni
aninditā saggamupenti ṭhānaṃ.

Never will a person of good conduct be blamed as long as he observes the eight precepts and keeps on making merits which is conducive to happiness. Such a person, equipped with morality, is sure to enter into the Realm of Bliss

189. Na vedā samparāyāya
na jāti napi bandhavā
sakañca sīlasaṃsuddhaṃ
samparāyasukhāvahaṃ.

Neither can the Vedas be of real help in the hereafter, nor can his birth nor relatives. Only his flawless morality can bring about the happiness in the hereafter.

190. Pahussutopi ce hoti
sīlesu susamāhito
ubhayena naṃ pasaṃsanti
sīlato ca sutena ca.

A learned man who is firm in his morality is praised both for his morality and learning.

191. Yo ca vassasataṃ jīve
dussīlo asamāhito
ekāhaṃ jīvitaṃ seyyo
sīlavantassa jhāyino.

A hundred years of an immoral and wavering person is not worth one day of a person who practises morality and concentration.

192. Sīlamevidha sikkhetha
asmiṃ loke susikkhitaṃ
sīlaṃ hi sabbasampattiṃ
upanāmeti sevitaṃ.

Do study the law of Morality. With morality well studied and observed in this world come all kinds of wealth.

193. Sīlaṃ rakkheyya medhāvī
patthayāno tayo sukhe
pasaṃsaṃ vittilābhañca
pecca sagge pamodanaṃ.

If a wise man hopes for the threefold enjoyment of fame, wealth and happiness in the hereafter, let him sincerely practise morality.

194 Sīlavā hi bahū mitte
saññamenādhigacchati
dussīlo pana mittehi
dhaṃsate pāpamācaraṃ.

One who practises morality, having his words and deeds well-controlled, will be befriended by many, while one who does not behave himself in accordance with morality, who is given to immoral conduct, will be shut off from his friend.

20. SEVANĀVAGGA – SECTION OF ASSOCIATION.

195. Asante nūpaseveyya
sante seveyya paṇḍito
asanto nirayaṃ nenti
santo pāpenti sugatiṃ.

Let not a wise man associate with the vicious. Let him associate with the virtuous. Because the vicious person will lead him to hell, while the virtuous person to the higher plane of existence.

196. Tagaraṃ va palāsena
yo naro upanayhati
pattāpi surabhī vāyanti
evaṃ dhīrūpasevanā.

Just as a leaf smells sweet when it wraps up a perfume herb, so does a man gain reputation when he is befriended by the wise.

197. Na pāpajanasaṃsevī
accantasukhamedhati
godhākulaṃ kakaṇṭāva
kaliṃ pāpeti attanaṃ.

He who keeps bad company cannot enjoy the absolute happiness. He inflicts evil upon himself. He is the same as an iguana in a flock of chameleons.

198. Pāpamitte vivajjetvā
bhajeyyuttamapuggale
ovāde cassa tiṭṭheyya
putthento acalaṃ. sukhaṃ.

Let him who hopes for real happiness keep away from bad company. Let him associate with the virtuous persons, and respectfully follow their instructions.

199. Pūtimacchaṃ kusaggena
yo naro upanayhati
kusāpi pūti vāyanti
evaṃ bālūpasevanā.

Just as a leaf has a rotten smell when it wraps up a rotten fish so is a person disgraced when he is befriended by the vicious person

200. Yādisaṃ kurute mittaṃ
yādisañcūpasevati
sopi tādisako hoti
sahavāso hi tādiso.

He is apt to be the same as his friend whom be associates with, for association has its nature as such.

201. **Saddhena ca pesalena ca**
paññavatā bahussutena ca
sakhitaṃ hi kareyya paṇḍito
bhaddo sappurisehi saṅgamo.

A wise man should associate with a pious person who is delighted with morality and who is bleseed with wisdom and knowledge, for it is a blessing to associate with such a person..

Printed at Mahāmakuta–Rāji–Vidyālaya Press,
Phra Sumeru Road, Bangkok, Thailand.

Nai Pinich Oosamrau,
Printer and Publisher
2501

CPSIA information can be obtained
at www.ICGtesting.com
Printed in the USA
LVHW080744220620
658684LV00008B/958

9 780344 999963